STOP ASKING JESUS INTO YOUR HEART

LifeWay Press®
Nashville, TN

ISBN: 9781430039747
Item number: P005720371

Dewey Decimal Classification Number: 242.5
Subject Heading: PRAYER \ CHRISTIAN LIFE \ BIBLE. N.T. GOSPELS

Printed in the United States of America

Student Ministry Publishing
LifeWay Church Resources
One LifeWay Plaza
Nashville, TN 37234-0144

We believe that the Bible has God for its author; salvation for its end; and truth, without any mixture of error, for its matter and that all Scripture is totally true and trustworthy. To review LifeWay's doctrinal guideline, please visit *www.lifeway.com/doctrinalguideline*.

CONTENTS

ABOUT THE AUTHOR 4

SESSION 1 **IMPORTANCE OF ASSURANCE** 5

SESSION 2 **JESUS IN MY PLACE** 17

SESSION 3 **UNDERSTANDING BELIEF** 29

SESSION 4 **UNDERSTANDING REPENTANCE** 41

SESSION 5 **CAN I LOSE MY SALVATION?** 53

SESSION 6 **EVIDENCE OF CHANGE** 65

NOTES 78

ABOUT THE AUTHORS

J.D. Greear At the age of 27, J.D. Greear became the pastor of a 40-year-old neighborhood church. In the 9 years since, that congregation of 400 has grown to over 5000 in weekly attendance. Today, the Summit Church, located in Raleigh-Durham, NC is recognized as one of the fastest growing churches in North America.

As a teacher, J.D.'s messages aren't intended to just show people how to live better lives. His goal is to leave people in awe of the amazing love of God. Because of his belief in the power of the gospel, J.D. has led the Summit to set a goal of planting more than 1000 gospel-centered churches in the next 40 years.

J.D. holds a Ph.D. in Systematic Theology from Southeastern Baptist Theological Seminary. He also lived and worked among Muslims in Southeast Asia for two years and wrote *Breaking the Islam Code*. J.D. and his beautiful wife, Veronica, have four ridiculously cute kids: Kharis, Alethia, Ryah, and Adon.

Unless God calls him elsewhere, J.D. plans on staying at the Summit Church until he preaches his last sermon at his own funeral before saying goodbye and hopping into the casket.

Jason Gaston is the student pastor at The Summit Church, located in Raleigh-Durham, North Carolina, and recognized as one of the fastest growing churches in North America. Jason received a Master's degree from Southeastern Baptist Theological Seminary in Wake Forest, North Carolina, and has been in full-time student ministry for eleven years. Jason's desire is to see a generation of students transformed by the gospel and living out that mission both locally and globally. Jason and his wife, Katie, are the parents of three children: Holt, Annie and Parks.

IMPORTANCE OF ASSURANCE

OVERVIEW

God wants you to be assured of your salvation.

That truth is essential to the life of every believer as they seek to follow Christ in obedience. But the sad truth is that many people struggle to know with certainty that they belong to Jesus.

In our opening session, J.D. Greear will discuss the uncertainty that often goes through our minds when we think about our salvation. This entire study is built around this simple question: *How can anyone know, beyond all doubt, that they are saved?*

Too many students who are truly saved struggle with doubt. They become spiritually paralyzed, spending time and energy worrying whether they've done enough to gain God's approval. They are locked up in fear, when they should be resting in the grace and promises of God.

The flip side of that coin, however, is that there are many who are living with false assurance of their salvation. They have bought into the notion that because they simply prayed a prayer, or walked an aisle, or held up their hand, that their place with God in eternity is secure.

This first session will emphasize God's desire for you to be assured of your salvation, and how assurance in the goodness of God will propel you to a lifelong journey of obedience and radical faith.

WARM UP

- **What are some phrases or terms you have heard centered around the salvation experience.**

- **If a friend were to ask you "What does it mean to be saved?", how would you respond?**

- **How would you define "assurance"?**

WATCH

Use this video guide to follow along with J.D.'s teaching. Fill in the blanks of the key statements, then use the additional space to note other important information.

- **The good news is that God does want you to know that you _____ to Him.**

- **God wants you to be sure of your salvation for a couple of reasons:**
  1. **He _____ you.**
  2. **We will never be able to thrive in the Christian life, to make bold _____, until we are assured of God's love for us.**

- **You're never going to be able to lean your life fully on Jesus, to take your hands off everything else, until you're confident of His _____ to you.**

- **Love for God only grows in the _____ of His love for us.**

- **This study is about . . .**
  - **. . . how for sure a person can know they're _____.**
  - **. . . how they can know for sure they _____ to Jesus.**
  - **. . . how they can know for sure Jesus _____ to them.**

VIDEO FEEDBACK

Use the questions below to help process the teaching you heard on the video.

J.D. stated in the video that he has prayed "the prayer" thousands of times, been baptized multiple times, and walked forward at youth events all over the country. How did that resonate with you?

Do you agree with J.D. that there are students that should have assurance of salvation that don't, and students who feel assured of their salvation, but shouldn't be? Explain.

Which of the key statements is the most important for you? Why?

If you could summarize the main point from the video in a tweetable statement (140 words or less), what would it be?

GROUP DISCUSSION

1. Read John 14:18. Just as J.D. mentioned, God does not want us to doubt his love. How does the idea of God being a faithful Father to the fatherless change the way you view Him?

   How has He been this for you?

2. When was a time you were assured of something and it motivated you to action?

3. Read Romans 8:15. What are the two categories of people mentioned in this passage? How are the two different?

4. How does knowing that God longs for you to know Him as "Abba, Father!" change the way you view him?

WRAPPING IT UP

God the Father longs for you to intimately know Him as a loving daddy. He does not simply want your service as a servant, but rather He longs that you would give Him the intimacy of a son or daughter. God wants for you to be assured of His love toward you. This entire study is built around the simple premise that God the Father wants you to be confident of His love for you and the salvation you have in Christ Jesus.

Are you part of God's family? Are you assured of His love? Explain.

What is one truth from this session that resonates with you?

What is one question that still troubles you?

REFLECT AND PRAY

As you close the session, focus your praying on the following requests:
  • Pray that your eyes would be opened to how God loves you.

  • Pray that you would move from being uncertain about your salvation to being assured.

  • Pray your heart would be overwhelmed with the love of God as a result of this study.

Key Thought: Assurance fuels the fire of obedience.

Read Daniel 3:1-12.

As young men, Hananiah, Mishael, and Azariah, were captured and taken to a distant land by their enemies. There they were subjected to a new language, new literature, and even given new names: Shadrach, Meshach, and Abednego. Though they found themselves in a foreign land among foreign gods, these three young men found great favor among the Babylonians and were even promoted to a place of great influence.

However, there came a point when these three young men had to make a difficult choice:

- Why was their choice so difficult? What was the looming penalty for disobeying the King's edict?

Read Daniel 3:13-23.

- What did they choose to do?

- How did these three young men display an unwavering faith in this situation?

Even in the face of death, they refused to bow to King Nebuchadnezzar because of their obedience to the One True God; Yahweh. They valued God's glory more than preserving their own lives.

- List their bold answer to the King here (vv. 17-18):

- What would prompt that kind of faith statement in the lives of these young men?

They had a great affection for and loyalty to God that was worth more than life itself. Fully assured of God's goodness toward them, they put their trust in Him, regardless of the situation or the outcome.

- Would you have done the same? Explain.

Read 2 Timothy 1:8-12.

- How was Paul able to remain focused and passionate about the mission in the midst of the suffering and persecution he faced in his life?

Paul was confident of his standing before God regardless of what life threw at him.

"You'll never give up your life in radical obedience until you are radically assured of His radical commitment to you." –J.D. Greear

Just like the rappelling illustration J.D. shared in the video, we need to be reminded that it is only when we come to a place of confidence and assurance in Christ that we will be moved from spiritual paralysis to spiritual freedom.

- In what ways have you found yourself spiritually paralyzed and not able to move forward in assurance in Christ?

"In the same way, there are points you can never pass spiritually until you are confident that Jesus will support the full weight of your soul. There are sacrifices you'll never make and commands you'll never obey unless you are convinced of their eternal value. Following Jesus, after all, means saying 'no' to a lot of things." –J.D. Greear

Read Matthew 16:24.
- What does it mean to take up your cross and follow Jesus?

The call to all disciples is a call to FOLLOW HIM and TAKE UP YOUR CROSS … it's a call to die to yourself and put your faith and confidence in Him.

"You'll never have the courage to embrace the cross until you have the confidence that you own the resurrection." –J.D. Greear

An assured faith fights off temporary fears for the promises of a faithful God.

Reflect and Pray
- Ask God to give you great confidence in His love for you and His passion to see you grow more into His image.

- Confess to Him areas where you have doubted His goodness and His ability to sustain you in all situations.

- Commit to live courageously as you trust in His faithfulness.

DAY 2 PERSONAL WORK

Key Thought: We are loved by God as intimately as a child, a spouse, and a friend.

His Beloved Child: Read John 14:16-18

* What promise did Jesus make to His followers? What was the significance of this promise?

As Jesus prepared to leave His disciples, He assured them that they would not be left alone. Can you imagine a loving and committed earthly dad just choosing one day to leave his children behind as orphans, never to see them again? Of course not!

Just as a good earthly father would never abandon his children, Jesus promised that He was not abandoning His followers. He promised that the Father was going to send the Holy Spirit to remain with them. That promise is still being fulfilled in our lives.

There is no doubt how much God loves us. His faithfulness and presence proves it.

His Spouse: Read John 14:1-3

* Where does Jesus say that He is going? And what does He promise to do?

Jesus promises that He is going to His Father's house to prepare a place for us. At first glance, this may seem insignificant, but J.D. pointed out that this would have brought to mind the imagery of a Jewish man going to prepare a home for his soon-to-be wife. It was an expression of his love and care for the one he loved. Our modern equivalency of this is when a man goes out to buy a diamond to put on his fiancée's hand. It lets everyone know, "She is mine, you can't have her, and my love is only for her."

His Friend: Read John 15:13-15

* What is the difference between the loyalty of a friend and the loyalty of a slave?

Both on the surface will probably get you a cup of water if you ask them to. The slave will do it because he fears what will happen if he doesn't obey. The friend will do it because he loves you and wants to do something pleasing for you.

- How do we know the depth of God's commitment to our relationship?

We see it in verse 13, that God laid down His life for us, that He sent His one and only son to die in our place.

- Which one of the previous relationships gives you the most assurance in your relationship with God? Why?

- Have you allowed an earthly version of these relationships to taint the perfect version we have in God? For instance, has a bad or absent father caused you to struggle to relate to God as a good and loving father? Explain

"The same love the perfect Father has for the perfect Son is the love that Christ, our everlasting Father, now has for us . . . But if the Son of God doesn't sit around wondering about His relationship to His Father, I should not be worried about my relationship to Him." —J.D. Greear

"I pray that you, being rooted and firmly established in love, may be able to comprehend with all the saints what is the length and width, height and depth of God's love, and to know the Messiah's love that surpasses knowledge, so you may be filled with all the fullness of God." Ephesians 3:17b-19, (HCSB)

- How does understanding the way God loves you change the way you live your life?

Reflect and Pray
- It is sometimes hard to imagine the depth of God's love for us because no one on earth has loved us with the same depth and consistency. Ask God to give you a greater understanding of His love.

- Ask that He would allow you to rest in His love and acceptance rather than seeking to earn it from Him or from others.

DAY 3 PERSONAL WORK

Key Thought: God wants our obedience to be from love, not fear.

God isn't looking for us to do what He wants because we are worried about what will happen if we don't. He doesn't want us constantly looking over our shoulders, worrying that the next time we mess up is the last time before He is tired of forgiving us. He wants us to obey Him because we love Him.

Read Romans 8:12-16.
- What type of spirit does this passage teach us we did and did not receive?

We have not received a spirit of slavery to fall back into fear. We have received the spirit of adoption as sons. A son loves his father and trusts that what the father asks him to do is good for him. His obedience is not motivated by fear, but love.

- What does the Spirit enable us to cry out?

As we discussed in the session, to understand God as loving Father was foreign to Paul's original audience. We can use the intimate term "Abba" (similar to our term "Daddy") because we have a Father who loves us enough to adopt us as sons and daughters at the cost of His only Son's blood.

Martin Luther pointed out that someone who obeys God out of fear and another who obeys out of love may look very similar on the outside. Fear can produce a "surface level adherence to the law."[1] But under the "thin-veneer of obedience will rush a river of fear, pride and self-interest."[2] The only way to have a real love for God is when our fear of Him is removed.

Read Romans 8:31-39.
- To what lengths did God go to remove our fear of Him?

God "did not spare His own Son." Pause for a moment and think about that. Who or what is most important or precious to you? Is there anything that you would give that up for? This is exactly what God did for us. He sent His one and only Son to live as a man, to be persecuted and mocked by the very people he created. Then, He was beaten and nailed to a cross, separated for a time from His Father whom He had known from eternity past. When we were far from Him, unable to save ourselves; God reached down to our helpless estate and set us free, adopting us as His own.

Look again at the following promises from these verses. What confidence does this give us to come before the Father?

- *"If God is for us, who can be against us?" –Romans 8:31b*
- *"He who did not spare his own Son but gave him up for us all, how will he not also with him graciously give us all things?" –Romans 8:32*
- *"Who shall bring any charge against God's elect? It is God who justifies." –Romans 8:33*
- *"Who is to condemn? Christ Jesus is the one who died—more than that, who was raised— who is at the right hand of God, who indeed is interceding for us." –Romans 8:34*
- *"For I am sure that neither death nor life, nor angels nor rulers, nor things present nor things to come, nor powers, nor height nor depth, nor anything else in all creation, will be able to separate us from the love of God in Christ Jesus our Lord." –Romans 8:38-39*

Even though we have heard many of these promises before and even though we acknowledge that God did not spare His own Son, we still often struggle to believe and rest in the assurance we have as God's children.

Read 1 John 5:10-13.

- What does John tell us the purpose of his letter is?

John tells us that our confidence and assurance comes from two things: belief in the testimony about eternal life, and the evidence of that eternal life at work in us.

"Eternal life is not just a reality we enter into when we die; it is something that comes into us now, and its evidences appear everywhere." –J.D. Greear

Reflect and Pray

- Pray that you would be set free from a fear of God's wrath. Pray that God would grant you the faith to believe that He has adopted you as a son or daughter, that He has set you free from wrath, and that nothing can separate you from His love.

- Call out to God as your "daddy" and ask Him to give you eyes to be able to see Him more clearly in this way.

2

SESSION TWO

JESUS IN MY PLACE

OVERVIEW

"Jesus suffered the full extent of God's judgment; all that is left for me is acceptance." —J.D. Greear

"Hope springs eternal in the human breast."

Those words from Alexander Pope in his "An Essay on Man," reflects the thought that even when it seems all is lost, hope can push us forward.

However, many times our search for hope leads us to things that will never satisfy: friendships, academic success, health, athletic promise, family stability, and more. While many of the things we place hope in are not wrong or sinful, the reality is that the things of this world will always fail at some point. Families fall apart. Health deteriorates. Athletes get injured. A friend lets you down.

The gospel is different. The gospel is not just an offer of hope to humanity; it is the only hope for humanity.

In session two, J.D. will remind us of the great work that Jesus completed on the cross, taking our place to become the atoning sacrifice for our sins. He will challenge us to believe the testimony concerning Jesus and place our hope in what He has done for us.

WARM UP

- **How would you define hope?**

- **What are some things you see students putting their hope in other than in Christ? Why do you think they turn to those things?**

- **Are you ever tempted to place your hope in something of the world? Why or why not?**

WATCH

Use this video guide to follow along with J.D.'s teaching. Fill in the blanks of the key statements, then use the additional space to note other important information.

• **The most important question that you will ever answer in any situation, in your entire life, is do you know for sure that you are _____?**

• **Jesus is our propitiation, which means He has absorbed the _____ for our sins.**

• **When Jesus stands before the Father, He is not arguing my innocence, He's arguing His _____.**

• **God could not punish me any more for my sins because He's already punished Jesus and it would be unjust for God to give two _____ for the same sin.**

• **The gospel in four words is _____ _____ _____ _____. That is the testimony that God has given you about what Jesus has done, and to be saved means that you believe that.**

• **There's really only two postures that you can take to the finished work of Christ, you can believe the testimony, or you can _____ the testimony.**

VIDEO FEEDBACK

Use the questions below to help process the teaching you heard on the video.

What is the testimony J.D. keeps referring to in the video?

J.D. said you could sum up the gospel in four words: Jesus in my place. How does that statement sum up the gospel?

Which of the key statements is the most important for you? Why?

If you could summarize the main point from the video in a tweetable statement (140 words or less), what would it be?

GROUP DISCUSSION

1. In 1 John 1:8, John writes "If we say, 'We have no sin,' we are deceiving ourselves, and the truth is not in us" (HCSB). What are some ways you have tried to suppress your sinfulness (make it out to not be as bad as you think it is)?

2. How does that keep you from seeing the truth of your sinfulness?

3. Read Isaiah 6:1-5. When Isaiah encountered the holiness of God, what was the first thing he realized about himself? Explain.

   Why is understanding your sinfulness so critical to experiencing salvation?

4. Review 1 John 2:1-2. In the first verse, Jesus is described as our advocate. In the second verse, He's described as the propitiation for our sins. What do those terms mean and why are they so critical to the gospel?

   When you understand what Jesus has done for you, what is your response?

We may not be worthy to be forgiven, but He is worthy to forgive us. —J.D. Greear

WRAPPING IT UP

There once lived a great king who ruled justly and lovingly over his kingdom. One day, it was discovered that someone had been stealing from the king's treasury. So, he issued an edict: "Whoever is found guilty will receive the just punishment of 10 lashings."

Again, someone stole from the treasury the next week. The punishment was now at 20 lashings.

The fifth week, the king set the punishment at 50 lashings. But when the guilty party was found, there was a problem: the one who had been stealing was the king's own daughter. The whole kingdom was on edge. Surely, the king wouldn't carry out the punishment.

On the day of sentencing, his daughter was tied to the stake. Just before the king gave the order, he wrapped his arms around his daughter, covering her body with his, then commanded, "Render the punishment." The king took the punishment for his daughter and satisfied the demand for justice. [1]

- **If an unsaved friend asked you to explain the phrase, "Jesus in my place," what would you say?**

- **What is one truth from this session that resonates with you?**

- **What is one question that still troubles you?**

REFLECT AND PRAY

- Have you believed the testimony about yourself that you are the person deserving of the wrath of the King because of your sin against Him? And have you embraced the testimony that Jesus was your sin bearer, absorbing the wrath of God on your account, so that you might know His love, grace, and forgiveness? That is where assurance of faith starts. It starts with a correct view of our sin, God's grace to us in Christ, and our belief in the gospel!

- Take a moment to thank God for the great salvation He has provided in Christ. Rejoice that He has taken your punishment and provided forgiveness for your sins.

DAY 1 PERSONAL WORK

Key Thought: We either believe the testimony of Jesus or we reject it.

Many professing Christians still struggle with the question of where they will spend eternity. Though they know the promises of Scripture about assurance of salvation, they still worry that when it comes down to it, they aren't going to get in. Perhaps most, if not all of us have wrestled with this at some point in our lives. Whether we think we've sinned too much, or our faith is not big enough, we can't seem to find peace.

Read John 3:36.
- How many categories of people do you see in this verse?

It seems clear that there are two categories of people – believers and non-believers. The HCSB actually says, "The one who believes . . . the one who refuses to believe." There isn't a middle ground for those who kind of believe, or those who believe but have really messed up. There are simply those who believe and those who don't.

- So, what are we supposed to believe in? What is it exactly that we our placing our hope and faith in?

Read 1 John 5:10-11.
- According to John, what is the testimony we are called to believe?

Notice that this means that eternal life is not found in ourselves. It isn't up to our ability to do anything.

"If we think that we have spiritual life in ourselves—that we are worthy of God's acceptance, or that we can be good enough to earn God's approval if we just try a little harder, or that God knows we are doing our best and will accept our good intentions—we reject God's testimony about the indispensability of Jesus and call Him a liar." —J.D. Greear

- What are some ways you reject God's testimony that eternal life and our acceptance is found in nothing other than Christ? Another way to think about this is, if you were to make a case before God about why he should accept you and let you into heaven, what would you say to him?

Many of us would tout our goodness, while others might try to stand on our religious activity. Regardless of what we would argue, ultimately we fall far short of the mark and even more disturbingly, make God out to be a liar.

If there was any other way for us to enter heaven besides God's own Son dying on the cross, do you not think God would have taken it? Of course he would have! He didn't just fail to think of something. Jesus' death provided the only way for us to be reconciled to God. It is our faith in that sacrifice alone that qualifies us and enables us to enter into the presence of a Holy God.

In the following verses, how is the message of the gospel summarized:

- **1 Corinthians 15:1-3**

- **Romans 10:9-10**

- **2 Corinthians 5:21**

The heart of the gospel is that we can't save our sinful selves, but God in His grace has made a way for us through the sacrifice of Christ. We respond to His grace with repentance and faith. And remember: it isn't the power of our faith that saves us, but the power of Who we are placing our faith in. It is God who saves completely. Nothing can separate us from His love.

Reflect and Pray
- If you have tried to make your case for salvation on anything other than faith in Jesus, confess that to God.

- Ask for the faith to believe in Christ's finished work on the cross to be the hope of your salvation.

- Thank God that it is what He has done for us that saves us.

DAY 2 PERSONAL WORK

Key Thought: Eternal life comes completely as a gift from God.

In the beginning, God created a perfect world and set us into it as His image bearers. We were set up to live eternally in the presence of God. However, we sinned and were cast out of the garden. So sin is not just what we do, it is a part of the human condition. We are born into it, as a disease that is passed down from our parents all the way back to Adam. Sin isn't just an activity (something we do), but an identity (who we are).

As a result, no amount of good activity counteracts sin. What we need is not more or better activity, but a new identity, and that can only come from outside of us.

Read Ephesians 2:1-5.
- What was our state or condition before Christ?

- What can a dead man do to bring life to himself?

Paul made it clear that we were hopeless, dead in our sins. There was absolutely nothing we could do change our condition. We needed someone outside of ourselves to come to our rescue.

Read 1 John 2:1-2.
- How does John make it clear that Jesus is the answer to our sin problem?

John states that when we do sin, Jesus is our advocate before God. And not only our advocate, but also the propitiation for our sins.

- What is an advocate?

An advocate is someone who goes to court on behalf of another to make their case for them. Usually the advocate argues for a person's innocence based on their good character or extenuating circumstances. Jesus doesn't do that. There is no argument there. We are guilty. So instead, Jesus argues on the basis of His righteousness in our place.

- What is propitiation?

Propitiation isn't a word that we use very often (or ever), but it means a claim that has been satisfied, wrath has been absorbed. Our sin was an offense to the holiness of God. In His holiness and justice, God's wrath had to come against the sin. It had to be paid for. Jesus took our place and absorbed that wrath, the full penalty for our sins.

"We were so bad he had to die for us: He was so gracious He was glad to die. When we repentantly believe that, we receive eternal life." —J.D. Greear

Read 1 John 1:9.
- What is the basis for God forgiving our sins?

John said God forgives based on His faithfulness and justice. Since Jesus has paid the full penalty for our sin, it would be unjust for God to punish us for that sin. God is always faithful to do that. It's not on a case-by-case basis.

- Not everyone turns to Jesus for the answer to their sin problem. What are some ways people try to deal with their sin outside of God's forgiveness?

Many people think they're good enough to make it, that their good deeds outweigh the bad. They look around and think they are better than most people and they hope that God will grade on a curve. Others make deals with God that if He will just forgive them, they will make it up to Him in the future. Others look to some place after death (purgatory) where they can work off their sin debt.

All of these ways reject what is made clear in the Scripture: there is one hope for sinners and that is the finished work of Christ.

Reflect and Pray
- Thank God that He has paid the penalty for our sin. Even though we were dead and helpless, He was glad to die for us in order to give us new life.

- Consider the people around you who need to hear the hope of this message. Pray that God would awaken their need for Him. And ask God for boldness and an opportunity to share the good news of the gospel with them.

DAY 3 PERSONAL WORK

Key Thought: Jesus + Nothing = Assurance

Read Hebrews 4:14-16.

- Who is our high priest and how is He described?

This passage tells us that Jesus is our great high priest. In the Old Testament, the high priest went before God on "the day of atonement," to offer a sacrifice for himself and for all of the people. It was an exacting process as the priest had to make sure he was completely clean to enter the presence of a Holy God. He would fast the day before, avoid touching anything unclean, bathe completely from head to toe, dress in all white, and then make a sacrifice. He would then come out, undress, bathe again, and go in again to offer another sacrifice. He would go through this whole process three times in order to make a sacrifice for himself, then the priests, and finally for all of the people.

Read Zechariah 3:3-9.

- How does Joshua the priest differ from the description of the high priest above?

On Yom Kippur, the high priest went to great lengths to ensure that he was completely undefiled and dressed in pure white. Joshua, on the other hand, is not just slightly dirty, but his clothes are covered in filth.

- How are we like Joshua?

No matter how much external cleaning we do, we can never clean our hearts of the sin that soils us. As the old saying goes, "you can put lipstick and pearls on a pig, but it is still a pig." No matter the lengths we go to change, only Jesus transforms us.

Through Christ, God has taken away our iniquity and given us His righteousness.

"Because Jesus, who deserved commendation, received condemnation instead, we who deserve condemnation can receive His commendation . . . you can summarize the gospel in four words: Jesus in my place." —J.D. Greear

Jesus in My Place

Read 2 Corinthians 5:21.

- What did Jesus take from us and what did He give?

Jesus not only took our sin upon Himself, but gave us His righteousness. In the book, *Stop Asking Jesus Into Your Heart*, J.D. illustrated this point by sharing how, as a broke Ph.D. student, he didn't bring much financially to his marriage. But when he married Veronica, he not only gained a wife, but a paycheck. Her income for her job went into their now joint bank account. J.D. didn't have to work for this money, but had access to it because of his relationship.

We often stress substitutionary aspect of Jesus' sacrifice, but often we don't talk about the "imputed righteousness" or the righteousness that was given as a result of what Christ did for us. It's as if we had a million dollars in debt. In reality, God not only paid the debt off for us, but He also credited our bank account with an additional million. We have the full righteousness of the Son of God Himself.

Read Romans 4:5.
Breaking the verse into three sections, list the importance of each of the phrases.
- " . . . to the one who does not work . . ."

- " . . . but believes in him who justifies the ungodly . . ."

- " . . . his faith is accounted as righteousness."

The person who doesn't trust in his goodness or works, but places his faith and hope only in Jesus, God will count this person's faith as righteousness. They will be washed clean by the blood of the Lamb and be given the full righteousness of Christ.

Reflect and Pray
- Thank God that He took your place, that through His death He took our sin and gave us His righteousness.

- Thank God that there is nothing you could do to ever make Him love you more and there is nothing you have done or will ever do that can make Him love you less.

- Continue to pray for the people you need to share the gospel with.

3

SESSION THREE

UNDERSTANDING BELIEF

OVERVIEW

"Biblical belief is the assumption of a new posture toward the Lordship of Christ and His finished work on the cross." —J.D. Greear

Believe. We hear that word a lot in our culture. Often, it's used in terms of motivation. Teams will use the phrase to rally their players around a common goal. Parents use it to motivate their children to pursue their dreams. Educators use it to push students out of apathy and focus on the great things that await them if they would only apply themselves. The list goes on and on.

But what does it mean in terms of our Christian faith? What role does belief play in the salvation and sanctification of every follower of Christ? How is belief more than just a feeling or emotion? Is mentally believing a truth about God simply enough?

In session three, J.D. will answer these questions and more as he unpacks what true biblical belief looks like according to Scripture. He will help you understand that assurance of salvation is not based on a past memory, but a present posture of repentance and faith.

WARM UP

- **How many decisions do you estimate you make in a day? Can you remember all of them? What's the most important decision you've made today? What's the most important decision you've made this week?**

- **In the space below, list all the things you did today that led you to the exact place where you are currently seated. Be as thorough as possible.**

- **Do you need to remember the day and the hour of your conversion to be absolutely sure you're saved? Why or why not?**

WATCH

Use this video guide to follow along with J.D.'s teaching. Fill in the blanks of the key statements, then use the additional space to note other important information.

- **People who have demon faith end up with a demon _____ . . . that is that even though they believe the right facts they are not going to be with God eternally forever.**

- **Belief does not become faith until you _____ on it.**

- **It is not a past memory, it is a present _____ that is the assurance of your faith.**

- **Saying a prayer is fine. It's just not the prayer that _____, it's the posture that the prayer signifies.**

- **Reducing salvation to a prayer ends up giving _____ to a lot of people who shouldn't have it and then keeping it from some who really should have it . . .**

- **The prayer expresses the posture of your heart which is _____ toward the Lordship of Christ and trust in His finished work on the cross.**

VIDEO FEEDBACK

Use the questions below to help process the teaching you heard on the video.

J.D. talked about understanding the moment of salvation as hopping up into the arms of Jesus as opposed to getting a certificate from Him. What did he mean by that?

How would you explain what J.D. meant when he talked about placing our hand of faith on Jesus?

Which of the key statements is the most important for you? Why?

If you could summarize the main point from the video in a tweetable statement (140 words or less), what would it be?

GROUP DISCUSSION

1. According to James 2:19, even the demons believe and they tremble. How would you define the belief of a demon? Is it saving faith? Explain.

2. Read Hebrews 10:39. There are two actions in this verse, one negative and one positive. What is the negative action? What is the positive action? How is this verse reflected in the lives of believers listed in Hebrews 11?

3. Paul tells the Roman Christians in Romans 10:9-10, that an essential element to true biblical belief is confession. What is the statement of confession that is at the heart of belief? What does it mean?

4. According to Mark 1:15, there are two actions that go together in true biblical belief. What are those two actions and why are they not separated?

"There is only one posture ever appropriate to Christ: surrendered to His Lordship, and believing that He did what He said He did."
—J.D. Greear

WRAPPING IT UP

Just as J.D. said in the video clip from this session, your present posture is better proof than a past memory. Salvation is a posture of repentance and faith toward the finished work of Christ, not simply a ceremony that you went through and received your certificate for entrance to heaven. Remember, it's about where you are currently seated rather than trying to remember if you ever sat down in the first place. If your current posture is not under the Lordship of Christ, simply repent and believe. Return to that posture of obedience.

- **Do you now have a better understanding of biblical belief? Could you explain it to your parents? To an unsaved friend? Explain.**

- **What is one truth from this session that resonates with you?**

- **What is one question that still troubles you?**

REFLECT AND PRAY

- Look back through this session and prayerfully consider what you have heard and studied.

- Evaluate. Is your faith saving faith? Are you in the posture of faith and repentance before the Lord?

- Take a moment to pray with a friend or a small group. Pray for each other that the truth you're hearing would be clear to you and your friends.

DAY 1 PERSONAL WORK

Key Thought: Repentance and belief are, biblically speaking, parts of the same whole.

Read Acts 16:28-31.
A great earthquake wreaked havoc on the prison where Paul and Silas were being held. The foundations of the prison were shaken, all of the doors were flung open, and the prisoners chains were loosened. The prison guard, knowing that an escaped prisoner would cost him his life, was astonished to find that not a single prisoner had escaped. Paul and Silas greeted him by saying, "Don't harm yourself, for we are all here."

This great and surprising act of kindness led the prison guard to ask, "What must I do to be saved?" Paul's response was simple: *Believe.*

We have noted that Jesus is to be the object of our belief. But now we turn to look at the nature of biblical belief.

Read Mark 1:14-15.
- What does Jesus say is necessary for salvation? How do you reconcile this with what Paul said in Acts 16?

Jesus isn't adding to the requirements for belief, but clarifying what real, biblical belief is. Belief in who God is and what He has done changes us and demands for us to live our lives in a different way. If Jesus is Lord and God sovereignly controls the universe, the only right response to Him is worship and obedience.

Read Hebrews 11.
This passage is commonly called the "Hall of Faith" because it recounts many of the Old Testament heroes and their faith. As you read, notice that their faith is not marked by a simple statement of belief, an intellectual assent to a core set of doctrines or "praying a prayer." Instead, Hebrews 11 identifies these heroes of the faith by their actions.

"Biblical belief is the assumption of a new posture toward the Lordship of Christ and His finished work on the cross." —J.D. Greear

It's not that statements of faith and the "sinner's prayer" are unimportant. For many, these expressions are vehicles whereby a posture of repentance and faith in the finished work of Christ is professed. However, these verbal expressions cannot just be seen as "get out of hell free" cards. You can't simply say some magical words and then go back to living however you please. If you have truly encountered the glory, holiness, goodness, and graciousness of God, you cannot walk away unchanged. Your whole life will be different.

- As you think about your own faith, list all of the things that you believe to be true about who God is? How do or how should these affect the way you live? Use the columns below. There are two examples of how to do this:

Character/Belief	Action
God is good	Even in bad times, we continue to seek the Lord and obey, knowing He is good and cares about us.
God is sovereign	I will not worry about my circumstances as if I was in control. I will trust that "God works all things out for the good of those who love Him (paraphrase)." Romans 8:28

Reflect and Pray
- Take some time and honestly examine the disconnect that exists in your life between what you say you believe and how you live your life.

- Spend time confessing and repenting of ways you have failed to live out your stated beliefs. Ask God to give you the faith to live out what you say you believe.

DAY 2 PERSONAL WORK

Key Thought: Becoming a Christian is not completing a ritual, but commencing a relationship.

When I was growing up, I remember watching shows about wizards and witches on television. Whenever they needed to cast a spell, whether to disappear or turn someone into a frog, they would go to their dusty, mahogany bookshelf, pull out their massive book of spells, turn to the page they needed and recite carefully and precisely the words needed to cast the spell.

Many people think that "getting saved" is a similar experience. The pastor from the front during the invitation asks us to bow our heads, fold our hands, and then repeat the words as he tells us the magic words to become a Christian. This ritual ceremony then gives us our "certificate" that we can show God when we get to heaven and tell him, "see God, I got the paper, I prayed the prayer, now let's party."

- What's the danger of basing your salvation on this type of experience?

This system works great until your memory fails you. Or you mess up really badly. Or you deceive yourself into thinking something happened that really didn't. Then, you start questioning if you really did enough or said the words in the right order or really meant it.

The better way to view your salvation is to picture yourself jumping into the arms of Jesus, submitting your life to His Lordship and trusting Him to take you to heaven. If you doubt, you could look back and try to remember the moment you jumped, but knowing when you began to rest is less important than that you are doing it now.

Your present posture is more important than a past memory.
–J.D. Greear

Read the following passages and note how the verbs in each are present and continual, not passive.

- John 10:27-28. *Christ's sheep are those who hear Him and those who follow Him.*
- John 3:36. *Whoever believes and whoever obeys is the one who sees eternal life. Inherent in obedience is an ongoing lifestyle change that continually looks to God for direction and guidance and follows accordingly.*

- John 9:36-38. *The man's belief leads him to worship Christ. This shows that belief not only leads to a posture of obedience affecting your will, but it also affects your heart, leading to a posture of worship.*

When I arrive at the movies, after I get my ticket and my gigantic tub of popcorn, I head into the theater and find the perfect seat, not too far forward that it hurts my neck or too far away that it is hard to see, not directly next to anyone and not behind the lady with the really big hair. Now, think about it, after I've gotten through the credits and the movie is started, how do I know that I've sat down in the chair? Sounds like a silly question, right? I don't think back through all of the choices that led to me sitting where I sat and try to make a case for how I know I am sitting. Of course not! I simply look down and see that I have taken my body weight off of my legs and placed it onto the chair.

When we examine our lives to see if we are "really saved," we don't need to flip to the front of our Bibles where we wrote down the date we accepted Christ. We simply need to look at our lives right now and ask the question, "Am I placing my faith and trust, the weight of my life, on Christ?" Remember, it's not past memory but present posture.

Read Leviticus 4:1-4.
- What did the placing of the priest's hand on the head of the bull symbolize?

By placing the weight of his hand on the bull, the priest, symbolically, transferred his sin and the sin of the people onto the sacrifice. Similarly, when we place our faith in Christ, trusting in His sacrifice, we are transferring our sin off of us and onto Christ.

"So, when it comes to assurance, the only real question is: Is your hand resting on Jesus' head now?" —J.D. Greear

- When it comes to your salvation, are you trusting a past memory or a present posture of faith and repentance?

Reflect and Pray
- Consider the sacrifice Jesus made for you. Consider the love He has for you that would compel Him to make that sacrifice.

- Spend time just thanking Him for who He is and what He has done for you.

DAY 3 PERSONAL WORK

Key Thought: While there is a moment of salvation, the ongoing posture of your life is more important.

Salvation does start at a specific time. There is a point in time when a lost person, dead in their trespasses and sin, crosses over from death to life by the saving work of Christ and the Holy Spirit. There is a distinct moment when that saving relationship with the Lord begins.

Each of the following passages speak of a transformational moment. Read each passage and record the moment.
- John 3:1-3

- Acts 22:16

- Colossians 1:13

Notice that each of these verses speaks of a specific time when a person is transferred to the kingdom of light, a time when sins are washed away, and a time when new birth takes place. For some people, that moment is a very vivid memory. That moment was accompanied with a dramatic change in the trajectory of your life. Others, like J.D. Greear, have grown up in church, came to Christ at a young age and prayed "the prayer" so many times that it is hard to nail down exactly when the actual moment of new birth was.

"The point is not whether we remember making the decision to get into the posture but whether we are in it now." —J.D. Greear

Read and summarize the following verses:
- Romans 4:3

- Romans 4:23-25

- Romans 10:9

We see from these verses that salvation is obtained simply by believing two things that God has promised: that Jesus died to pay the penalty for our sins and that He was resurrected as proof of God's acceptance of that sacrifice. Just as Abraham believed and it was credited to him as righteousness, we too simply place our faith in the finished work of Christ and trust God to hold true to His promise to us.

"Don't try to find assurance from a prayer you prayed in the past; find assurance by resting in the present on what Jesus did in the past. If you are resting right now in what Jesus did two thousand years ago to save you, then, if never before, you are saved at this moment . . ." —J.D. Greear

Read Ephesians 2:4-10.

Twice in this passage Paul reminds us that it is by grace alone that we have been saved. He tells us that it is a gift of God and not the result of our works. While what we do does matter, even verse 10 tells us that we are created and prepared for good works, but it is not the good works that save us. If there was anything at all that we could do to earn our salvation, then it would follow that there was something that we could do to lose it. And as a result, we would never be able to have assurance.

But, because our salvation is by faith alone, through Christ alone, a free gift from God, we simply have to accept it and it is ours, forever! As we continue on in a posture of belief and repentance, we can have unwavering certainty that God is our Father and we have eternal life in Him.

Reflect and Pray
- Go back to Ephesians 2:1-10. Spend time praying through the content of this passage.

- As you read verses 1-3, confess the wickedness of your own heart to God and look at your sin not just as breaking rules, but as harming a relationship.

- Then, as you read verses 4-10, praise God for who He is, what He has done, and who He has made you to be in Him.

4

SESSION FOUR

UNDERSTANDING REPENTANCE

OVERVIEW

"We don't come to him as bad people trying to become good people; we come as rebels to lay down our arms." —C.S. Lewis

Repentance can seem like a burden. It's as if God's relentless anger toward us overwhelms our souls to a point where we have no choice but to repent. From a Christian perspective, that's a faulty view. Repentance for the follower of Christ is not a burden, but rather the kindness of God that leads us to Him (Rom. 2:4). The problem with repentance is not the act of repenting, but rather the false assumptions we have in regard to what true repentance actually looks like.

In this session, J.D. will help us understand what repentance is and what it is not. Let's face it, we all need a little clarification on the what and why of bringing all of our dirt before the Lord.

WARM UP

- **Describe a time when you had an "aha" moment that brought clarity to a situation.**

- **Have you had any of those moments with this study? Explain.**

- **Repentance is more than just being sorry you got caught. Agree or disagree? Explain.**

WATCH

Use this video guide to follow along with J.D.'s teaching. Fill in the blanks of the key statements, then use the additional space to note other important information.

What repentance is not:

• Repentance is not a motion of your hands, feet, or mouth. It is a motion of your _____.

• Repentance is not just feeling _____ for your sins.

• Repentance is not just _____ of your sin.

• Repentance is not just getting religiously _____.

• Repentance is not just partial_____.

• Repentance is not _____.

What repentance is:

• Repentance is absence of a settled _____ toward God.

• Repentance is not just stopping sin, it's starting to _____ Jesus.

• Repentance is a genuine Spirit-filled change of _____.

VIDEO FEEDBACK

Use the questions below to help process the teaching you heard on the video.

Look back over the misconceptions about repentance. Which of these has confused your understanding of repentance in the past? Explain.

Summarize in your own words what repentance is.

Which of the key statements is the most important for you? Why?

If you could summarize the main point from the video in a tweetable statement (140 words or less), what would it be?

GROUP DISCUSSION

1. **Read Luke 15:11-21. In what ways did the prodigal son demonstrate genuine repentance?**

2. **Read 2 Corinthians 5:17 and Galatians 2:20. How do these passages describe someone who has experienced salvation?**

3. **Repentance is not just a flight from sin, but pursuing something greater. Read 2 Timothy 2:22. How do Paul's instructions to Timothy illustrate this truth?**

"The desire to desire God is the first echo of a heart awakened to God." —J.D. Greear

4. **What is partial surrender? Why is it an inadequate response to God? In what areas of your life do you see evidences of partial surrender?**

5. **Read Psalm 86:11 below:**
   Teach me your way, O LORD, and I will walk in your truth; give me an undivided heart, that I may fear your name. (NIV)

   What does it mean to have an undivided heart? How do you experience this in your life?

"Belief in the gospel is not demonstrated by "never falling" but by what you do when you fall." —J.D. Greear

WRAPPING IT UP

Repentance is not merely praying a prayer, feeling sorry for your sin, or partially surrendering areas of your life to God. Repentance is, on the other hand, a change of mind, affection, and direction. Remember, it is God's kindness (not anger) toward us that leads us to repentance.

It's been said that many people who claim to be Christians will miss heaven by eighteen inches, the distance between the head and the heart. Don't let that be you. Let what you know to be true about Christ captivate your soul and command your behavior. Repent.

- **How would you explain repentance in one statement?**

- **What is one truth from this session that resonates with you?**

- **What is one question that still troubles you?**

REFLECT AND PRAY

Martin Luther once said that "all of the Christian life is repentance."

- What do you think that means?

- How have you been deceived about repentance in the past?

- If you've never repented of your sins and placed your faith in Jesus, do so now.

- If you're already a follower of Christ, but have fallen back into sin for a season, take time now to repent of your sin and turn your life back to Jesus.

Key Thought: Repentance is recognizing Jesus as Lord.

Read Luke 14:26 and 14:33.

- What does Jesus ask of those who want to become his disciples? Does this seem overly harsh to you? Explain. Why would Jesus ask this of us?

To follow Jesus calls for complete and total surrender. That's what it means for Him to be Lord. If He is truly Lord, then our love for and allegiance to Him must rise above all others. This doesn't mean we literally have to hate our mother or father. It is clear from other passages that we are to respect and obey our parents (for example, Eph. 6:1). What Jesus is saying is that our love and admiration for God and the way that we submit to Him should be so strong that all other love and relationships pale in comparison.

- -

"We don't come to Him as bad people trying to become good people; we come as rebels to lay down our arms." —C.S. Lewis

As we come to Christ, we don't come as people who are pretty good and just need a little extra boost to become better. We come as people who need a complete makeover, people who are on the opposing team who switch sides completely. As we do this, we come to Jesus with the recognition that He is Lord. This is the posture of repentance.

Read the following verses and note the common theme:
- Mark 1:14-15
- Acts 2:37-38
- Acts 17:30-31

In each of these passages, repentance is called for. In Mark, Jesus' first sermon calls people to "repent and believe." In Acts 2, Peter's sermon at Pentecost calls for the people to "repent and be baptized." Later in Acts 17, Paul is speaking to a crowd in Athens and he says the old times are gone and God has made it clear that "all people everywhere [are] to repent."

It is important for us to realize that "repentance is not subsequent to belief; it is part of belief. It is belief in action—choices that flow out of conviction.[1]"

Read John 3:36.

- What connection does John make between belief and obedience?

John tells us that the two are so closely linked that they are interchangeable. There is no one who believes that does not also repent and obey. To believe means to come to Jesus as complete Lord over every single area of your life, no matter how small.

So, does that mean that until we turn 100% of our lives over to Christ that we are still not truly Christians? Of course not! If that was true, Jesus Christ would be the only Christian. Belief means that we have started the journey with Jesus. Repentance is simply the ongoing recognition of areas where we fail to submit and surrender. Every believer will struggle with this. As J.D. points out in the book, *Stop Asking Jesus Into Your Heart*, "Didn't even the greatest saints have blind spots . . . Didn't Peter deny Jesus at one point? . . . King David committed adultery and murder and then lied about it for several months." Of course these aren't models to emulate. They are examples of broken, sinful, imperfect people who God loved, called, and used for His purpose. They are examples that give us hope in the midst of our brokenness and failure.

Reflect and Pray

- Similar to our prayer time in the first Personal Work of Session 3, spend some time specifically confessing areas, of your life that you have yet to surrender to God. In each of these areas, ask yourself, what am I not believing about God that leads me to disobey Him? For example, if you struggle with seeking approval from others, the root of this weakness lies with not believing you are accepted by God and knowing that your relationship with Him is enough. If you struggle with sexual sins, you are not believing that God's timing and the satisfaction found in Him is enough for you.

- Identify and confess these areas of unbelief. Ask for God to help you believe what's true about Him, and rest in His goodness and graciousness.

DAY 2 PERSONAL WORK

Key Thought: Understanding repentance starts by understanding what it is not.

To remind us of what true repentance is, let's review the six common misconceptions we looked at in our last group session.

1. Repentance is not simply a prayer that we pray. It isn't a card we fill out and it isn't just simply telling someone else we messed up. These things may be helpful, but at most they are the evidence of repentance, not the act itself.

2. Repentance is not just feeling sorry for our sin.

Read 2 Corinthians 7:10-11.

- What does Paul say distinguishes godly grief from worldly grief, and what does he say is the result of each?

Paul says that godly grief produces a repentance without regret that leads to salvation. He says this kind of grief is filled with an earnestness and eagerness to change. Worldly grief may look like godly grief on the surface, but it doesn't lead anywhere. There may be shame and embarrassment over what happened, and regret that you got caught, but no life-change accompanies this grief. There is no desire for change, no heart for repentance. This leads to death.

3. Repentance is more than the confession of sin. In the video, J.D. shared about the dynamics of the climactic summer camp invitation. He says by the end of the week, after lots of sermons and little sleep, the emotional dam would finally break. It would start with one girl, spread to a few others, and eventually, whole groups of girls would come up front crying and confessing everything they had ever done.[2]

Confessing our sins to others can feel purifying, but often times people are just looking for someone to tell them they are okay. But "even confession of our sin to Jesus, soaked with tears, but apart from a change of attitude toward our sin, will not bring about eternal life.[3]" Our confession must lead to repentance and true change will be evidenced by the fruit it produces, not the amount of our tears.

"Our tears do not wash away our sin. Only Jesus' blood does."
—J.D. Greear

4. Repentance is not "getting religious." Often times people think that repentance is about doing more things for God. This results in a Christian checklist. They start reading their Bible and praying daily, being nicer to people, they may even start serving somewhere, thinking if they do enough good stuff they will be able to keep God off of their back and clear their conscience.

Read 1 Samuel 15:22-23.
   • What does God delight in from us?

God is much more interested in our obedience than He is in our religious activity. He doesn't want us to view Him as someone we need to get off our backs and leave us alone so we can get back to our lives. He wants our affection and our obedience. To use J.D.'s illustration, "a cheating man who buys his wife expensive gifts is not addressing his unfaithfulness but covering it up.[4]" Often times this is how we treat God.

"Repentance is not securing a pardon before God so that we can go on sinning with impunity; it is a choice to submit to God and to seek ceasing from sin entirely." —J.D. Greear

5. Repentance is not partial surrender. Many people want to give God certain areas of their lives and then look to him for advice in others. As J.D. said, we often view God as we do our navigation system. We input the destination and the system provides a route to get there. If we chose a different route, the system recalculates accordingly. God doesn't recalculate according to our whims. He wants full and total surrender. Partial surrender is no surrender at all. If God is not Lord of all, He's not Lord at all.

6. Repentance is not perfection. As we looked at in the last lesson, God does not expect us to be perfect.

Read Romans 7:22-24.
We see Paul here recounts the inner struggle that all of us have. None of us will be perfect this side of heaven. Strive for holiness, pursue Christ, but realize you won't be perfect.

Reflect and Pray
   • As you look through the list of things that repentance is not, ask God to help you overcome any of the false ideas and beliefs that you have held. Confess times when you've experienced worldly grief instead of godly grief. Ask God to give you a true heart of repentance that desires holiness.

Key Thought: True repentance turns from sin, follows Christ, and begins to hunger for God.

1. Repentance is the Absence of Settled Defiance

Read the following verses and list what characterizes the righteous:

- Luke 6:46-48

The person who can walk through the storms of life and not be destroyed is the one who obeys what God commands. This person builds their life on the foundation of the Word of God.

- Proverbs 24:16

Living the godly life doesn't mean that we never fail or mess up. It means that when we do inevitably fail, we don't stay down, but get up, confess and repent, experience God's restoration and continue to follow Him.

"Belief in the gospel is not demonstrated by "never falling" but by what you do when you fall." —J.D. Greear

We need to remember that as we commit to a life of repentance, we are not entering a life of fewer struggles, but actually inviting more struggles into our lives. While some people have miraculous conversion stories of being addicted to drugs, accepting Christ, and waking up the next day free from their addiction, this does not seem to be the norm. For most people, following Christ is committing to a life-long battle against sin.

2. Repentance is not just stopping sin, but starting to follow Jesus.

Read the following verses. Note the key idea in each one.
- Mark 8:34-35

- Deuteronomy 10:12-13

- Micah 6:8

All of these verses indicate that loving God and following Him is not a passive existence. It's not about just stopping a few of our bad habits. When I was in high school, I thought I was a good Christian because I didn't use profanity, I didn't sleep around, and I didn't drink. I looked good to the church crowd and I patted myself on the back. It wasn't until later that I grasped that following Christ is about much more than what we don't do. It is about a passionate pursuit to be holy as He is holy, and to know and love Him more deeply.

3. Repentance is a Spirit-filled change of desire.

Read 2 Corinthians 5:17.

- What does Paul tell us about who we are in Christ?

God actually makes us a new person with new desires when we invite Him into our lives. The Holy Spirit dwells in believers to empower them and enable them to love the things God loves and hate the things God hates. Again, this change is not instantaneous freedom from ever sinning, but we have been give the desire to pursue holiness.

Jesus repented in my place. Read Matthew 3:1-17.

How can we know if we have repented enough? J.D. stated that Jesus was baptized so that all righteousness would be fulfilled. Since Jesus had never sinned, the righteousness He was fulfilling was not His own, but ours. In Christ, we find both the forgiveness of our sins in His death, as well as the perfect life on our behalf through His time on the earth. We don't have to repent perfectly, He did that for us.

Reflect and Pray
- Review each of the previous points. Pray through each one asking God to help you understand true repentance.

- Pray that you would be unsettled about sin you may have grown comfortable in. Ask God to bring that sin to mind, then repent of it.

- Consider what steps you need to take to devotedly follow Jesus. Give Him complete control of your life. Finally, thank God that He has perfectly done what you could not on your own, and rest in that truth.

CAN I LOSE MY SALVATION?

OVERVIEW

We live in a world of tensions. Tension is simply the coexistence of two opposing ideas or elements. Healthy tension comes when those things work together in such a way that brings about clarity.

In the Bible, there seems to be tension around the doctrine of salvation. There are several passages that back up the idea that once someone is saved, they will always be saved. Yet at other points in Scripture, you see statements such as "You will be saved if you hold on until the end." On the surface, this looks like irreconcilable tension, but it's not. This tension has been the subject of many conversations in Christian circles for centuries and it is still prevalent today.

In this session, J.D. will show us that the tensions that we perceive in these passages are actually not tensions at all. We'll see how these two ideas work together. Rather than two currents of water working against one another, they seem to be two currents of water running together in the same direction.

WARM UP

- **When was the last time you felt like quitting something, but instead pressed on and endured to the end?**

- **What were the emotions, tensions, and feelings you experienced that made you want to quit? How did you feel when you endured to the end?**

- **Do you think you can lose your salvation? Why or why not?**

WATCH

Use this video guide to follow along with J.D.'s teaching. Fill in the blanks of the key statements, then use the additional space to note other important information.

- **See to it, brothers, that none of you has a sinful, unbelieving heart that turns away from the living God . . . We have come to share in Christ if we hold firmly until the _____ the confidence we had at first. (Heb. 3:12,14)**

- **One of the evidences of saving faith is not the intensity of the emotion at the beginning, but how it _____ to the end.**

- **It is true that once saved always saved. But it is also true that once saved, forever _____.**

- **Faith that fizzles before the finish is _____ from the first.**

- **Assurance in the Bible is always given to those whose belief is in the _____ tense.**

VIDEO FEEDBACK

Use the questions below to help process the teaching you heard on the video.

How would you have responded to the guy in J.D.'s opening story?

What does it mean for your faith to endure to the end?

Which of the key statements is the most important for you? Why?

If you could summarize the main point from the video in a tweetable statement (140 words or less), what would it be?

GROUP DISCUSSION

1. **Read Matthew 13:3-9. What does the seed represent in this passage? What are the different soils the seed falls on? What do they represent?**

2. **In the video, J.D. stated "the evidence of saving faith is not the intensity of emotion at the beginning, but it's endurance over time." How do you see that played out in the parable of the sower in Matthew 13?**

3. **Read Matthew 10:33; Revelation 2:7; Revelation 2:11; Hebrews 3:12-14. What is the common language you hear in these passages?**

Praying a prayer to ask Jesus into your heart, even if it's followed by a flurry of emotional and religious fervor, is no proof that you are saved. Enduring in the faith until the end is. —J.D. Greear

4. **Read 1 John 5:18. How does John speak to the issue of assurance of salvation?**

WRAPPING IT UP

Remember, a faith that endures to the end always takes the posture of repentance throughout your life. When you find yourself in seasons of life where you are pursuing sin and not the righteousness of God, the way back to the Father is through repentance and faith. That is what it means to "forever follow" Christ.

- **So, if someone asked you to explain the belief, "once saved, always saved," how would you explain it? How has this session helped you clarify the issue?**

- **What is one truth from this session that resonates with you?**

- **What is one question that still troubles you?**

REFLECT AND PRAY

- As believers, we are called to finish strong. Are you a strong finisher? Why or why not?

- Evaluate. Pray and ask the Holy Spirit to give you clear understanding about your relationship with Him. Are you walking closely with Christ? Are you in a backslidden state and needing to repent? Or are you yet to make a first-time decision to follow Christ through faith and repentance? Remember Christ stands ready to meet your need.

- If you are a follower of Christ, thank God for saving you and ask Him for the grace and strength to sustain you until the end.

DAY 1 PERSONAL WORK

Key Thought: The nature of saving faith is that it always endures to the end.

Last session we discussed how people are confused by the fact that the Bible speaks of eternal security for the believer, yet also often warns us about falling away from the faith. In order to reconcile these two ideas, let's look at what the Bible has to say.

Read the following verses. Write the promise found in each verse:
- John 6:37-39

- John 10:27-28

- Romans 8:29-30

These promises speak clearly. We can be confident that those who God has called to Himself, those who know Christ and follow Him, can be certain of their salvation.

If this is the case, then why so much confusion? It seems some of the uncertainty comes from the language we have used to describe salvation. When we reduce salvation to just saying a prayer, followed by a promise that saying the words guarantees you for eternity, we provide false hope. In a way we've said heaven is a certainty regardless of what you do with your life. But that's not the truth of Scripture.

Read the following verses. Write the conditional statement about salvation found in each verse.
- Philippians 2:16

- Romans 11:22

- Hebrews 12:15

- John 15:6

According to Scripture, there is more to our assurance and the Christian faith than just saying a prayer, getting our name in the Lamb's book of life and moving on. We must continue to seek after Christ, abiding in Him, and following His Word.

Read the following verses. Note the key feature of a saving faith in each verse:

- Matthew 10:22

- Revelation 2:7

- Revelation 2:11

"Faith that fades, no matter how luscious its firstfruits, is not saving faith." —J.D. Greear

While at first glance it appears that these passages are teaching that we can lose our faith, they are actually teaching the nature of saving faith. It isn't that some people's faith makes it to the end and others don't; it's that true, saving faith, always makes it to the end.

"A true believer can never be lost, but a true believer also will never stop following Jesus". —J.D. Greear

Stay strong. Endure to the end.

Reflect and Pray
- Stop and examine your salvation. Is it based on the finished work on Christ? Have you transferred the weight of your soul upon Jesus? Or are you basing it on a prayer you prayed at some point. Again, not that the prayer is wrong. But it isn't the prayer that saves you. It's repentance and faith in what Christ has done for you on the cross. That faith will carry you to the end. Not that you won't struggle with sin. You will. But the struggle with it is proof of the new nature within you. It is the loving Father continuing to call you back to Himself.

- Thank God for the great salvation He has given you and for the security of that salvation that is found in Him.

Key Thought: If you reject the cross, there is nothing more that can be done. If you accept the message of the cross, you can be confident of your salvation.

Hebrews 6:4-6 is perhaps one of the most difficult passages in all of Scripture to understand. On first reading, the passage seems to indicate that you can fall way from Christ, and that if you do, you can never come back.

Let's look at the passage more closely. Start by reading Hebrews 6:4-6.

General Warning, Not an Individual Diagnosis
The first thing to note is that the author is speaking generally to a congregation and not specifically to an individual. When using phrases like "once been enlightened," "tasted the heavenly gift," and "shared in the Holy Spirit," he's speaking about actions that apply to the whole movement in the church, not just one individual. Everyone in the church, in some way, had experienced these things. But in every congregation there are people who join in the movement of God, but never experience true conversion. They may look like they are totally bought in, but in reality, they never experienced true transformation. So when things get tough, or the situation changes, they fall away. Their faith fizzles because it wasn't real.

- Recount some of the ways you have seen God move through answered prayer, lives being changed, blessings He has given, etc. Stop and pray, thanking God for the opportunity to experience His power, and acknowledge that what you have experienced is true and that your faith is in Him for the long run.

The Endurance of Saving Faith
The second important thing to note is this passage reinforces the truth that saving faith is enduring faith.

"Many go through the initial motions of salvation, yet, after a period of time, fall back into their old ways. Such a person was never really saved to begin with . . . " —J.D. Greear

Read Luke 8:13.
- **What type of person is Jesus describing here?**

Like the people described in Hebrews 6, these people receive the gift with joy. But over time, when the trials of life come and they are tested, they fall away.

Those Who Fall Away

The statement of "those who fall away cannot be renewed again to repentance" is difficult to swallow. Does that mean that every person who falls into sin for a season was never saved and has no hope? No. A helpful thing to remember when faced with a difficult passage is that since Scripture is unified and does not contradict itself, we should look to the more clear passages to interpret the less clear ones.

Using this method, we see throughout Scripture many examples of people who fell into sin and were restored:

- Abraham lied twice about his wife Sarah, telling Pharaoh that she was his sister. Yet, we see him as a hero of the faith, the father of the faith.
- David committed adultery and tried to cover it up by murder. But when he repented he was restored (2 Sam. 11—12).
- John Mark abandoned the mission he had when it got difficult and yet we later see him working again with Paul (Acts 13:5,13).
- And in 1 Corinthians 5, Paul described a situation where a man was sleeping with his mom. The church discipline instructions Paul gave the church were to help restore the man.

It is clear from these examples that God is constantly pursuing and patient with those who fall into sin. So, what is the author saying?

He's implying that if someone has truly seen the truth and experienced the power of God, but chosen to walk away, what's left to draw them back? If they've seen the convincing truth of the cross and the resurrection, but chosen to go back to the life of intentional sin, what else is left to convince them? If God sending His own Son to die in their place isn't enough to convince them of His love and their forgiveness, then nothing will. They're not coming back.

However, we can't know the spiritual condition of anyone other than ourselves. The only time we can know the Spirit is no longer speaking to someone is when they are dead. Until then, we are responsible to pray and they have the opportunity to repent.

Reflect and Pray

- Are you at a point where you think you've sinned so bad or so long that you can't be restored? That's not true. Repent now and enjoy the restoring love of Christ.

- Does this describe someone you know? Don't give up on them. Continue to pray for them and ask God to give you opportunity to encourage them to come back to Him.

Key Thought: God gives both warnings and assurances because both are necessary for Christian growth.

As we have seen in the previous studies, the assurance of our salvation doesn't come because we have signed an ironclad contract with God. Instead, the assurance of our faith comes from our present posture toward God. While the saying "once saved, always saved" is true, it is also true to say "once saved, forever following."

- -

"Faith that fizzles before the finish was flawed from the first."
—J.D. Greear

Read the following passages. Note the appeal the author gives in each passage.
- 2 Peter 1:5-10

Peter presents a list of characteristics that mark those who are following Christ. As you persist in these qualities and see them evidenced more and more in your life, this will help assure you of your salvation.

- Philippians 2:12-13

Notice Paul didn't say they were to work for their salvation, but to work it out, to put it into practice. They could do that through the power of God in them who would carry out His purpose for them.

But what if I backslide?

As J.D. says in the book, every Christian backslides. Every time we sin, we are turning from God and pursuing something else. The question people usually have is how long can I backslide before I conclude my initial profession of faith wasn't real?

That's a tough question. Scripture does not clearly answer. For some people, their conversion experience was so unmistakable and their venture into sin so brief that their past salvation experience was obviously genuine. For others though, because there was little life-change with their initial decision, and because the gospel really came alive for them later in life, the later experience probably was the conversion point. And for others, the moment of conversion is not obvious either way.

Fortunately, knowing the moment of conversion is not essential. Remember, the most important thing is not a past memory, but the present posture.

"At the end of the day, knowing the moment of your conversion is not essential. What is essential is to know that you are currently in a posture of repentance and faith." —J.D. Greear

As you consider your posture, ask yourself:
- Are you looking to Christ to lead you, or are you still in control of your life?
- Are you asking how you can please God, or are you asking how can He make your life better, easier, happier, etc.?
- Would you be happy in a world without pain, without sin, and with no worries, even if God was not there?

These questions will help you check your heart to see if you are using God and religion as a means to an end or if you have given control of your life over to Him.

Assurances and Warnings

So, what is most important, the assurances of Scripture or the warnings? Which should we focus on ourselves and which should we tell to others?

The answer, as you might guess, is both. We need the assurance of our faith to trust that God is good and loving. To know that even when we fail we can turn back to God based on His grace and mercy and not our works. To know that nothing can ever separate us from the love of God. To be secure in the truth that Christ is enough for life and salvation.

But we also need to heed warnings of Scripture to keep us from being complacent. To remind us it's not about our goodness or good works. To examine what it is we are living for and how we can grow in our pursuit, knowledge, and love of Christ. To compel us to warn others who may be basing their assurance on the wrong thing.

The warnings and the assurances work together to bring us closer to Christ.

Reflect and Pray
- Thank God that we have the assurance in Christ that there's nothing we can do to make Him love us more and nothing we can do to make Him love us less.

- Take a moment to consider the posture you're in. If you're far away from the Lord, repent and return to Him. If you are resting in Him, consider how you need to be growing in your knowledge of and service to Him.

6

SESSION SIX

EVIDENCE OF CHANGE

OVERVIEW

"Saving faith proves itself not only by persevering to the end, but also by the evidences of a love for God and a love for others." —J.D. Greear

A dog has just eaten something that could potentially be damaging to their intestines. So, the dog does what any good dog would do, they begin the vomiting process. They purge the bad stuff and you think it's over. But in totally disgusting fashion, the dog returns to its vomit and begins to have lunch. Nasty, right? That's actually what the Book of Proverbs tells us it's like when someone who loves God keeps on going back to the same sin. Where is the evidence of change in the life of a person that keeps on repeating the same sin over and over?

The Scripture actually points to some pretty strong evidences that someone's life has been changed by the gospel. When someone has encountered the living God of the universe, there is no way that they can ever walk away the same. There must be change. You see this with men like Isaiah in his encounter with the living God in Isaiah 6. You see it again in the New Testament with the Apostle Paul when he's on the road to Damascus and has an encounter with Jesus Himself. When you encounter Christ, your countenance and your character change.

In this session, J.D. will point out the evidences of a life changed by the gospel, and how they prove themselves in terms of internal posture and external behavior.

WARM UP

- **What does the phrase, "Where there's smoke, there's fire," mean?**

- **What is evidence?**

- **Consider for a moment . . . If you call yourself a Christian, what evidence do you see of that in your life?**

WATCH

Use this video guide to follow along with J.D.'s teaching. Fill in the blanks of the key statements, then use the additional space to note other important information.

• **When God saves us, He's not simply trying to get us to act a certain way, He's changing our _____. He wants us to be new people on the inside who begin to obey Him, not because we feel like we have to, but because we desire to.**

• **God gives us a new nature, and that new nature becomes a _____ that God is within you.**

• **If your best friends don't know that you have been born again, there's a good chance that you're _____.**

• **The most important thing for you to remember is to always go back to the posture of faith and repentance that you have toward the gospel. It is essential that you not base your assurance on your _____.**

• **So when you're in a place where you're looking in your heart and you're discouraged at how little you seem to have grown in godliness, in that moment you rebelieve the _____ . . . the gospel that Jesus has paid for all of your sins and that God does not accept you on the basis of how righteous you become, but on the basis of His finished work in Christ.**

• **So wherever you are, whatever situation you are in, whatever the diagnosis of your spiritual condition is, the _____ is the same: believe the gospel.**

VIDEO FEEDBACK

Use the questions below to help process the teaching you heard on the video.

J.D. pointed out the two main evidences of a life changed by Christ. What are they?

J.D. stated that if your best friend and your mom can't tell you've been born again, you probably haven't. Do you agree with that? Why or why not?

How often do you get the "faith, fact, feeling" out of order? Why do you think that's the case?

Which of the key statements is the most important for you? Why?

If you could summarize the main point from the video in a tweetable statement (140 words or less), what would it be?

GROUP DISCUSSION

1. Read 1 John 2:3-8. According to John, what are the evidences of someone that knows Christ?

2. Read 1 John 2:15-17. What does John say about how who/what you love is an evidence of salvation?

3. According to 1 Timothy 6:11-12, what does Paul instruct Timothy to do? According to that same passage, how would you characterize "fighting the good fight of faith," that Paul describes to Timothy?

4. Read 1 John 3:14-16. How does this passage reflect a similar truth from the Matthew 18 passage?

5. Read Matthew 18:23-35 as a group. According to Jesus, what are the evidences of someone who has a changed heart?

"Just as Christ has been to me, so I too will be to others."
—J.D. Greear

WRAPPING IT UP

Remember, you're not called to be perfect. There will be days when you stumble, sin, and don't feel much love for God. There will be days the grace and love you're supposed to express toward others will be replaced with impatience and irritation. At that point, you're not feeling much love toward others. Remember, don't feel your way into your beliefs, believe your way into your feelings. Let your faith drive your feelings, rather than letting your feelings drive your faith.

- **There are two major evidences that our hearts have been changed by the gospel: a greater love for God and greater love for people. Does your heart reflect these things?**

- **What is one truth from this session that resonates with you?**

- **What is one question that still troubles you?**

REFLECT AND PRAY

As you close out this study, pair up with another student and spend some time sharing and praying together:
- Discuss the struggles you've had with assurance of salvation and how this study has helped you.
- Talk about how you see or don't see the two evidences of salvation in your life.
- Ways in which you both can continue to fight the good fight of faith. How you help each other have faith that endures to the end.
- Spend time praying for friends who do not yet know Christ.
- Pray for each other to keep your eyes on Christ and that you would keep believing even when your feelings try to drown out your faith!

DAY 1 PERSONAL WORK

Key Thought: We have proof we are in Christ when we love God and love others.

When we are in Christ, there is a noticeable difference in our lives. It may not be instant and it may not be dramatic, but there is a recognizable difference in our lives. Even if our actions don't change too much, the motivation behind what we do does. For example, before becoming a believer, we may have avoided sin because we didn't want to get caught and get in trouble. But once we are in Christ, we avoid sin because we know it affects our intimacy with God.

Scripture shows us two categories of heart change that evidence our salvation: our love for God and our love for others.

A Love for God
Read the following passages. Note the evidence of salvation that each passage mentions.

- 1 John 2:3-6

If you love God, you'll do what He says.

- 1 John 2:15

You can't truly love God and love the world.

- 1 John 2:29 and 1 John 3:6

If you love God, you won't continue to disobey Him. You'll live a righteous life.

Again, striving to love God more and avoid sin isn't done in order to save ourselves or to impress God. We love God and obey Him because of what's He done for us and in us. We have a new heart, a new affection; one that wants to please God because we are in love with Him.

"Once God has given you an appetite for Him, you won't need to be forced to seek Him." —J.D. Greear

A Love for Others

Read 1 John 3:14-16.
- What characterizes the life of someone who follows Christ?

A sign that you are a true follower of Christ is that you love His people.

Read Matthew 18:23-35.
- What is so astonishing about this story?

- What point is Jesus making about our own salvation?

When we understand how much we have been forgiven, our response is to forgive.

Ask yourself the following questions:
- Do you struggle with being selfish with your possessions? How does understanding God's generosity in the gospel address this?
- Is your greatest desire in life to become rich, famous, and obtain all of your dreams? How does understanding Christ's sacrifice address this?
- Do you struggle to forgive others or tend to hold grudges? How can remembering God's forgiveness help you to love and forgive others?

"The sign that you have experienced grace is that you become gracious. Patience, forgiveness, generosity, delight in and compassion toward others are inevitable fruits of the gospel root." —J.D. Greear

Reflect and Pray
- Pray an entire prayer without asking for anything for yourself. Spend some time reflecting on the sacrifice, forgiveness, and grace found in God's love for you.

- Spend some time praying for the needs of others around you. Pray both for those who are in Christ and those who need to know His saving love.

DAY 2 PERSONAL WORK

Key Thought: The strongest evidence of our growth in grace is our understanding of our need for grace.

But what if we still struggle with sin? What if we still sometimes find it more pleasurable than following Christ? If God has given us a new heart and a new desire for Himself, then why do we still love to sin so much?

Our struggle with sin is real and only ends when we see Christ. However, it isn't necessarily something that should discourage us.

Read Romans 7:15, 19.
- Describe the struggle Paul speaks of in these verses.

- Can you relate to this struggle? Explain.

- Read Romans 8:1-4. What encouragement does Paul give in this passage?

It may sound contradictory, but the fact that we feel guilty over our sin and are continuing to struggle with it can actually be a good thing. Our uneasiness about our sin is actually a sign that we are not okay with sin being present in our life. It is an acknowledgment that sin is wicked and that we were created for more than what it offers us. The presence of God's Spirit inside of us points out the wickedness of sin and doesn't allow us to be content to continue in it.

Read 1 Timothy 1:15-16.
- Why would Paul say that he is the worst or chief of all sinners?

While it isn't explicit in the text, Paul was probably basing his "worst of all sinners" title not comparing himself to others, but comparing himself to the glory of God. As he saw more of God, he saw more of his sin.
- Are you tempted to compare yourself to other sinners and say, "I'm not that bad" or do you compare yourself to the holiness of God? Explain.

As we grow in our love and knowledge of God, we will inevitably see our sin more clearly. Think about when you finally get around to cleaning out your room. The slightest thing out of place is instantly noticeable. Similarly, as we come to know the holiness and perfection of God more, we begin to understand with greater clarity our own sinfulness.

"The more I have grown in Christ, the more (not less) I've felt my sinfulness. The more God's light has illuminated my heart, the more I've been able to see how messed up I really am." —J.D. Greear

Read Hebrews 3:12-14.

- What does this passage encourage us to do?

We are to be in community together, encouraging one another.

- How does being in community encourage and protect us?

- Do you have others that speak honestly into your life? When is the last time you asked someone to point out sin in your life? When is the last time you confessed sin to someone else?

We are not meant to be "Lone Ranger" Christians. We are to be involved with the community of believers called the church. Other believers can encourage us, pray for us, stand with us, and hold us accountable. They can help us see sin in our lives that we are blind to or have grown accustomed to. The writer of Hebrews helps us understand how much we need each other. Do not miss out on the great blessing of being involved in the church.

Reflect and Pray

- Confess to God your struggle with sin. Thank Him for His continued love, grace, and patience with you.

- List the sins you constantly struggle with. Pray, asking God to replace your desire for these things with a desire for Him. Then confess them to someone who you can trust and have them commit to praying for you as well.

- Thank God for the blessing of the church. Pray specifically for people in your church who love you, encourage you, and hold you accountable.

DAY 3 PERSONAL WORK

Key Thought: You don't have to feel forgiven to be forgiven.

As you come to the end of the study, perhaps you're still struggling with doubt. What do you do if you still don't feel like you are forgiven and you begin to worry if you are really saved? Here are three final truths to lean on when you have doubts.

1. You can rest in the Gospel.
Read Hebrews 4:8-11.
- What is the difference between the two types of rest mentioned in verse 8?

- What does this passage call us to strive for?

The rest that Joshua was leading God's people to, namely the promised land, was a type of rest, but not God's final rest. As is clear from the Old Testament, this rest was temporary, but pointed us to a greater final rest. The second type of rest is the final rest of the gospel found in Christ. We experience this rest now as we walk with Him and grow in Him. Then we will experience the rest fully when we go to heaven.

"On your very best of days, you must rest all your hopes on God's grace. On your worst of days, He should be your refuge and hope."
—J.D. Greear

2. God's prescription is the gospel.
Read Colossians 2:6-7.
- How do we continue to grow in our faith?

- What are some tangible ways that you can remind yourself of the gospel throughout the day? What are some ways to reflect on the gospel when you are having doubts?

When you are struggling with discouragement and doubt, dig into the Word. Scripture memory and meditation on God's truth can remind you of the character of God. Spend time in prayer, honestly unloading your heart before God. Allow the Spirit of God to minister to you in this time. Lean of godly friends in your community of faith. Share your struggles and allow them to encourage and pray for you.

Martin Luther said, "To progress is to always begin again.[1]" As you grow in the gospel, you will constantly become more aware of your sin. This will cause you to grow as you trust in God's grace and forgiveness even more. The faith that led you to believe in Christ for the first time and the faith that causes you to grow is the exact same thing. Both rest entirely in the gospel.

3. You don't have to feel forgiven to be forgiven.
The enemy will use our feelings against us. Our feelings will lead us astray and make us doubt our standing before God. The problem with feelings is they are extremely fickle. They can change so quickly, usually influenced heavily by our present circumstances.

Read 1 Corinthians 1:30.
- Where is our righteousness found and why should this reassure us?

Our righteousness is found in Christ, not in ourselves. As a result, it doesn't matter what we do or how we feel. Our righteousness is as secure as Christ's standing before His father in heaven. It is eternal, unshakable, and constant.

Reflect and Pray
- Do you sometimes let your feelings drive your assurance? What happens when you do that? Ask God to help you stand on your faith in Him, not on your feelings.

- As you close out this study, reflect back on all of the promises that Scripture gives us about our assurance in Christ. Reflect on the lengths God went to through Christ to bring us to Himself. Reflect on the fact that we don't have to be "good enough" to earn God's love. That life isn't a constant struggle and guessing game to see if we have done enough. Allow these truths to lead you to praise God and rest in the assurance that only the gospel can bring.

FOOTNOTES

SESSION 1
1. *Stop Asking Jesus Into Your Heart,* p. 22
2. *Stop Asking Jesus Into Your Heart,* p. 22

SESSION 2
1. *Gospel Prayer Leader Guide,* p. 10

SESSION 4
1. *Stop Asking Jesus Into Your Heart,* p. 55
2. *Stop Asking Jesus Into Your Heart,* p. 58
3. *Stop Asking Jesus Into Your Heart,* p. 59
4. *Stop Asking Jesus Into Your Heart,* p. 60

SESSION 6
1. *Stop Asking Jesus Into Your Heart,* p. 107

NOTES